S POTLIGHTS

AIRCRAFT

Written by Bob Munro

SIMON & SCHUSTER
YOUNG BOOKS

ACKNOWLEDGMENTS

Illustrated by
Don Simpson
Gary Slater
Gerald Witcomb

Picture credits
15 Lufthansa-Bildarchiv

First published in 1993 by
Simon & Schuster Young Books
Simon & Schuster Limited
Campus 400
Maylands Avenue
Hemel Hempstead
Herts HP2 7EZ

Planned and produced by
Andromeda Oxford Limited
11-15 The Vineyard
Abingdon
Oxon OX14 3PX

ISBN 0-7500-1418-0
Printed in Singapore by Kim Hup Lee

CONTENTS

INTRODUCTION

Each day, all over the world, thousands of airliners take off and land at airports large and small. How do they do it? How does an aircraft with hundreds of passengers on board manage to take off on time, fly for thousands of miles without getting lost, then land safely in bad weather and maybe even at night? This book answers all of these questions by taking you through a typical flight. It then looks at the many different types of aircraft that you can see at any airport you might visit. It also looks at helicopters, gliders and some of the world's more unusual aircraft.

HOW TO WATCH

There are many people who go to airports to watch aircraft. Most of them collect the registration carried by each aircraft, making a note of where and when it was seen. A pair of binoculars is very useful when doing this, as is a pen and pad to record the registrations. There are various books available at airport bookshops which allow you to look up a registration and find out what type of aircraft you have seen and who it is operated by.

INTRODUCTION
Concise yet highly informative, this introduces the reader to the events and equipment shown. This broad coverage is complemented by more detailed exploration of particular points in the numerous captions.

HEADING
The subject matter of each spread in this step-by-step guide to today's civil aviation is clearly identified by a heading prominently displayed in the top left-hand corner.

DETAILED INFORMATION
Captions with clear pointers to the illustrations provide a wealth of extra information to help appreciate the world of aviation.

LANDING

Approximately 30 minutes before arrival, the pilots prepare for the most dangerous part of the flight – landing. Speed is reduced and a descent is started. As the airliner gets closer to the airport, it is placed into a well-ordered landing pattern by an approach controller as other airliners may also be waiting to land. The flaps and undercarriage are lowered as the pilots concentrate hard on making a good approach and landing. Spoilers, autobrakes and thrust reversers help slow the airliner on the runway, and soon it is making its way to a gate at the end of the flight.

LANL
There
along
a pilo
white
appr

FLA
Flap
of t
low
b
the
he

LOOK OUT FOR THESE

THRUST REVERSERS
To help the aircraft slow down after it has landed, doors called buckets clam together at the back of each engine. This deflects the exhaust forward.

20

SPOTLIGHTS
A series of illustrations at the bottom of each page encourages the reader to look out for easy-to-spot equipment and events associated with civil aviation and airports around the world. Each is accompanied by a short description.

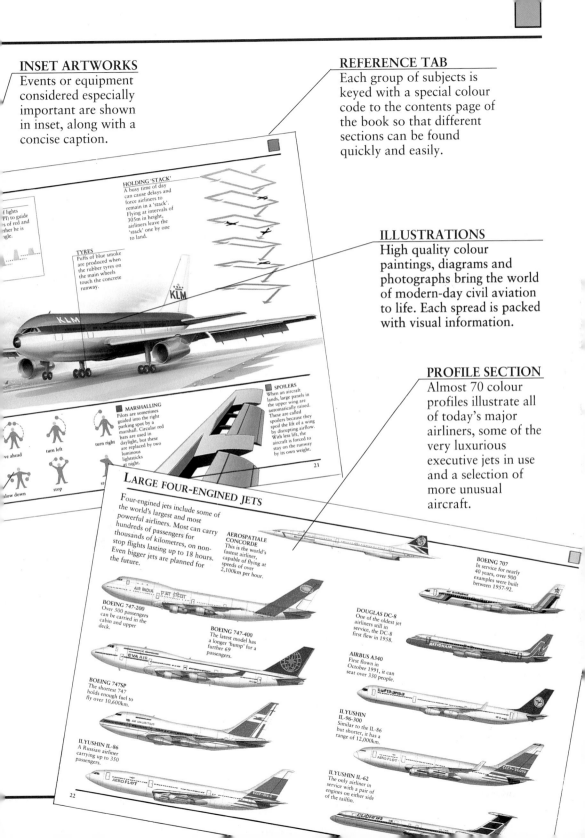

INSET ARTWORKS
Events or equipment considered especially important are shown in inset, along with a concise caption.

REFERENCE TAB
Each group of subjects is keyed with a special colour code to the contents page of the book so that different sections can be found quickly and easily.

HOLDING 'STACK'
A busy time of day can cause delays and force airliners to remain in a 'stack'. Flying at intervals of 305m in height, airliners leave the 'stack' one by one to land.

f lights
PI) to guide
s of red and
ther he is
gle.

TYRES
Puffs of blue smoke are produced when the rubber tyres on the main wheels touch the concrete runway.

ILLUSTRATIONS
High quality colour paintings, diagrams and photographs bring the world of modern-day civil aviation to life. Each spread is packed with visual information.

MARSHALLING
Pilots are sometimes guided into the right parking spot by a marshall. Circular red bats are used in daylight, but these are replaced by two luminous lightsticks at night.

SPOILERS
When an aircraft lands, large panels in the upper wing are automatically raised. These are called spoilers because they spoil the lift of a wing by disrupting airflow. With less lift, the aircraft is forced to stay on the runway by its own weight.

ve ahead turn left turn right

low down stop

21

PROFILE SECTION
Almost 70 colour profiles illustrate all of today's major airliners, some of the very luxurious executive jets in use and a selection of more unusual aircraft.

LARGE FOUR-ENGINED JETS
Four-engined jets include some of the world's largest and most powerful airliners. Most can carry hundreds of passengers for thousands of kilometres, on non-stop flights lasting up to 18 hours. Even bigger jets are planned for the future.

AEROSPATIALE CONCORDE
This is the world's fastest airliner, capable of flying at speeds of over 2,100km per hour.

BOEING 707
In service for nearly 40 years, over 900 examples were built between 1957-92.

BOEING 747-200
Over 500 passengers can be carried in the cabin and upper deck.

BOEING 747-400
The latest model has a longer 'hump' for a further 69 passengers.

DOUGLAS DC-8
One of the oldest jet airliners still in service, the DC-8 first flew in 1958.

AIRBUS A340
First flown in October 1991, it can seat over 330 people.

BOEING 747SP
The shortest 747 holds enough fuel to fly over 10,600km.

ILYUSHIN IL-96-300
Similar to the IL-86 but shorter, it has a range of 12,000km.

ILYUSHIN IL-86
A Russian airliner carrying up to 350 passengers.

ILYUSHIN IL-62
The only airliner in service with a pair of engines on either side of the tailfin.

22

BOARDING

Modern airports are designed to make travel easy. Before boarding the aircraft, all passengers have their tickets checked and they hand over large luggage to the airline staff. Passengers must show their passports at Customs and be passed by security. Hand luggage is passed through a detector which can identify dangerous items. Meanwhile, the airliner is cleaned, refuelled and restocked with food and drink. The passengers are only allowed on board when the crew and aircraft are ready to taxi to the runway for take-off.

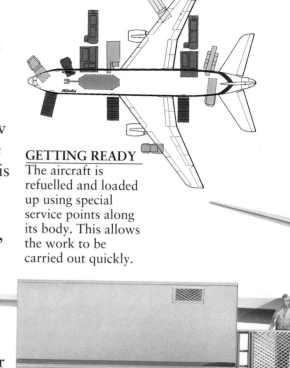

GETTING READY
The aircraft is refuelled and loaded up using special service points along its body. This allows the work to be carried out quickly.

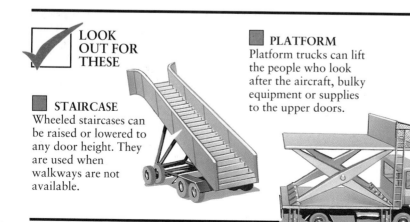

SERVICE VEHICLES
A variety of special vehicles surround the aircraft to load the passengers' luggage and food.

LOOK OUT FOR THESE

STAIRCASE
Wheeled staircases can be raised or lowered to any door height. They are used when walkways are not available.

PLATFORM
Platform trucks can lift the people who look after the aircraft, bulky equipment or supplies to the upper doors.

FORK LIFT
Fork lifts are also used to lift food and drink containers and heavy goods on to the aircraft.

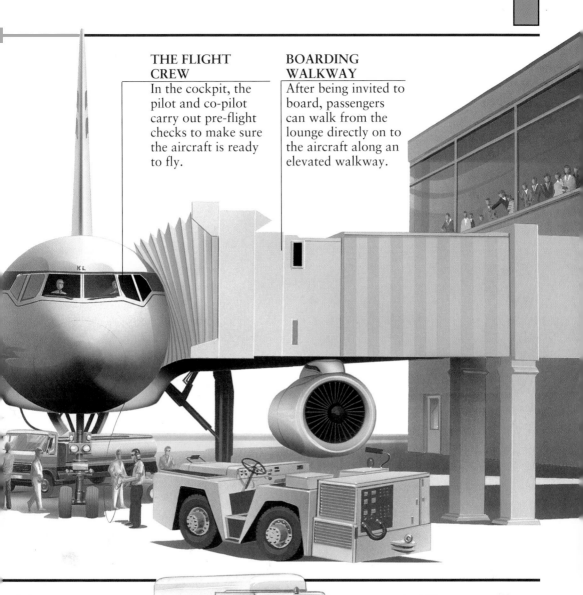

THE FLIGHT CREW

In the cockpit, the pilot and co-pilot carry out pre-flight checks to make sure the aircraft is ready to fly.

BOARDING WALKWAY

After being invited to board, passengers can walk from the lounge directly on to the aircraft along an elevated walkway.

■ **CONVEYOR BELT**
Luggage is loaded on to a conveyor belt, which moves it up and into the luggage hold of the aircraft.

■ **FUEL BOWSER**
Large airliners can carry thousands of litres of fuel. The fuel bowsers carry fuel to the aircraft.

■ **LOW LOADER**
Large, long and heavy objects are carried to and from the cargo hold of the aircraft on low loaders.

TAXIING

While the passengers find their seats, stow their hand luggage and fasten their seat belts, the pilot and co-pilot complete the pre-flight checks. Then they tell air traffic control that they are ready for departure. Outside, the tow-bar of a tug has been attached to the

THE ENGINES
When the engines are turned on, the blades of the airflow fan at the front of the engine begin to turn.

nosewheel. When air traffic control gives permission for the aircraft to leave the gate, the tug gets to work. In the cabin, the air hostesses or stewards demonstrate how to use the emergency equipment.

THE PUSHBACK TUG
With the long tow-bar attached, the driver of the tug starts to push the aircraft away.

LOOK OUT FOR THESE

■ PUSH–OUT TUG
Some tugs are used to help park airliners into awkward positions, ready for loading passengers or servicing.

■ HEAVY TUG
This powerful tug sits low on the ground to let it manoeuvre under any airliners which have a short nosewheel leg.

■ BIRD SCARER
To stop birds being sucked into the engines, bird scarers make a lot of noise to make the birds fly away.

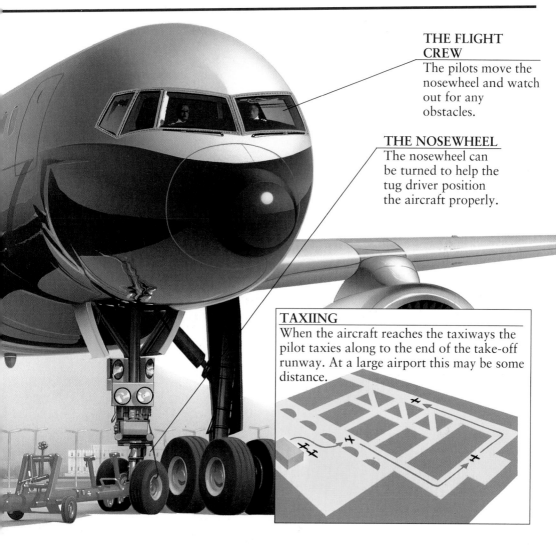

THE FLIGHT CREW
The pilots move the nosewheel and watch out for any obstacles.

THE NOSEWHEEL
The nosewheel can be turned to help the tug driver position the aircraft properly.

TAXIING
When the aircraft reaches the taxiways the pilot taxies along to the end of the take-off runway. At a large airport this may be some distance.

FIRE ENGINE
Large, powerful fire engines can reach a crashed aircraft in a matter of seconds. They spray a thick fire-retardant foam.

TRAFFIC CONTROL
With so many vehicles and aircraft moving around, some vehicles patrol the airport, making sure there are no accidents.

TRACTOR
Small tractors are used to tow several luggage carts at one time to and from the hold of an aircraft.

11

AIR TRAFFIC CONTROL

Without the men and women of air traffic control (ATC) it would be impossible for airliners to taxi, take-off and land safely. The pilots have to follow very strict rules if accidents are to be avoided, and it is the air traffic controllers who ensure the right rules are followed at the right times. Having given permission for the aircraft to start-up, pushback and taxi, air traffic controllers keep a watchful eye on the airliner as it heads off to wait at the runway holding point.

WINDOWS
It is important that the controllers can see the runways clearly. The windows are therefore tinted and angled to reduce glare.

PLANNER
The pilot contacts the ground movement planner for permission to start-up. The planner talks to the pilot via a radio link and headphones.

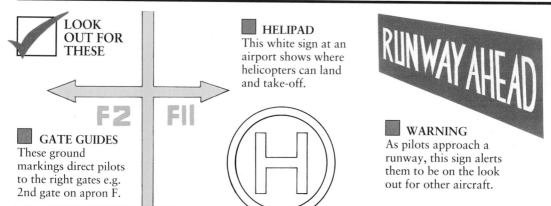

LOOK OUT FOR THESE

HELIPAD
This white sign at an airport shows where helicopters can land and take-off.

RUNWAY AHEAD

GATE GUIDES
These ground markings direct pilots to the right gates e.g. 2nd gate on apron F.

F2 F11

WARNING
As pilots approach a runway, this sign alerts them to be on the look out for other aircraft.

CONTROLLER

The ground movement controller gives the permission to taxi. Binoculars help him watch the aircraft.

CONTROLLER

At another console, a take-off and landing controller will give permission to enter the runway when safe.

CONTROL TOWER

High off the ground, the large windows of the visual control room gives a 360° view.

61-1 72-1

■ **SECTORS**
Long taxiways at big airports are divided into sectors so ATC knows exactly where each aircraft is.

■ **INSTRUCTION**
This sign tells the pilot to stop here and wait for permission from ATC to move on to Runway 31.

HOLD RW 31

09R CAT III

■ **CAT III**
Runways that have this sign have sensors that aircraft instruments can detect. These guide planes in to land in foggy conditions.

TAKE-OFF

Once the pilots have received permission to enter the runway from air traffic control, they line up the aircraft for take-off. When clearance is given, the captain pushes the thrust levers forward, releases the brakes, and the aircraft begins to speed up. 'V one', calls the co-pilot, indicating the speed at which the aircraft will take-off. When he calls 'Rotate', the captain pulls back on the control yoke until the nose lifts off the ground. Soon the co-pilot calls 'V two', indicating that the speed is high enough for the aircraft to safely take-off.

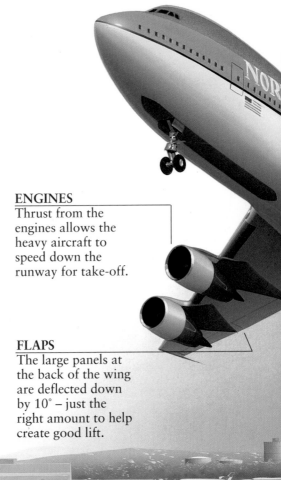

ENGINES
Thrust from the engines allows the heavy aircraft to speed down the runway for take-off.

FLAPS
The large panels at the back of the wing are deflected down by 10° – just the right amount to help create good lift.

LOOK OUT FOR THESE

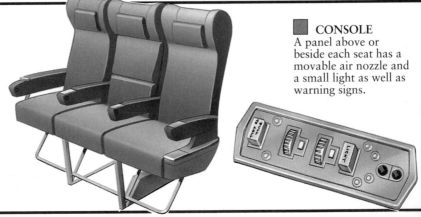

■ **PASSENGER SEATS**
Built to be strong but comfortable, the seats can be tilted back when the passenger wants to rest.

■ **CONSOLE**
A panel above or beside each seat has a movable air nozzle and a small light as well as warning signs.

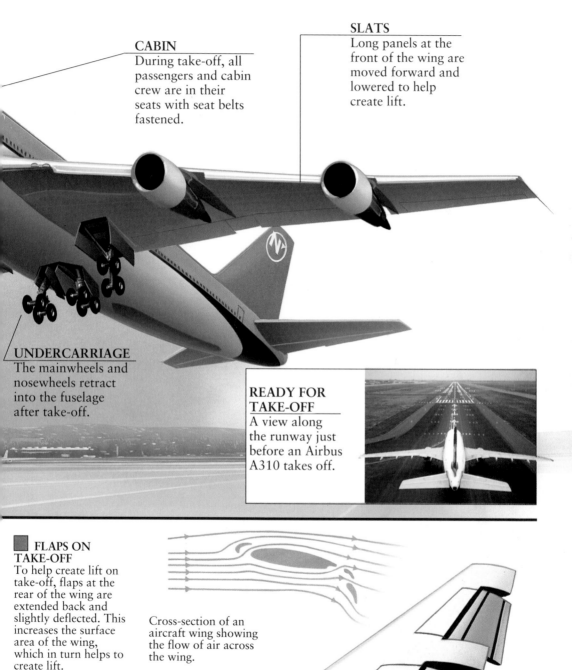

CABIN
During take-off, all passengers and cabin crew are in their seats with seat belts fastened.

SLATS
Long panels at the front of the wing are moved forward and lowered to help create lift.

UNDERCARRIAGE
The mainwheels and nosewheels retract into the fuselage after take-off.

READY FOR TAKE-OFF
A view along the runway just before an Airbus A310 takes off.

FLAPS ON TAKE-OFF
To help create lift on take-off, flaps at the rear of the wing are extended back and slightly deflected. This increases the surface area of the wing, which in turn helps to create lift.

Cross-section of an aircraft wing showing the flow of air across the wing.

IN FLIGHT

With the undercarriage and flaps retracted, the aircraft begins a series of climbs to its cruising height. This is usually between 9,150m and 11,285m. In modern airliners, much of the work is done by computers and autopilots, but the pilots must monitor the small TV screens in front of them and keep a look-out for other aircraft. In the main cabin, meals for the passengers are soon being prepared. The pilots will eat different meals, so that if one gets food poisoning, the other can continue to fly the aircraft.

INSTRUMENTS
Modern airliners include a series of small TV screens, which display all the flight data in full colour at the touch of a button.

PILOTS
The pilot (captain) always sits in the left seat, and the co-pilot (first officer) in the right. They wear headphones with intercoms for communication.

LOOK OUT FOR THESE

PILOT'S CAP
As part of their uniform, pilots wear a peaked cap with a set of gold wings.

EPAULETTES
Pilots wear gold shoulder bars. Three bars, for example, indicate the rank of first officer.

JACKET CUFFS
Gold bands are also worn on each sleeve. A captain or senior pilot has four bands.

SEAT LOGOS
Headrest covers on passenger seats often bear the airline's tail logo.

AIR CORRIDORS
Between airports the airliner usually flies within a set 'corridor' of air space. It is about 16km wide.

WINDSCREEN
The windscreen is made of large panels. A good view ahead and to the sides is very important for pilots.

CREW SEATS
Because the pilots may be sitting in them for many hours, the seats are built to be comfortable.

PASSENGER SEATS
The number of seats across a cabin in an airliner depends on its width, and the size and arrangement of seats to be fitted inside. A modern wide-bodied airliner will have between six and 10 seats across divided by two walkways (aisles).

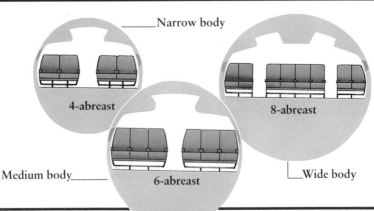

Narrow body

4-abreast

Medium body

6-abreast

8-abreast

Wide body

TRACKING THE FLIGHT

At all times during the flight, the aircraft is monitored by air traffic control, whose job it is to ensure safety in the skies. Each flight is tracked by radars on the ground, while radio beacons help keep the aircraft in the centre of its airway. Radio transmitters and receivers are used to relay communication between the air traffic controllers and pilots. The controllers' instructions must be obeyed at all times.

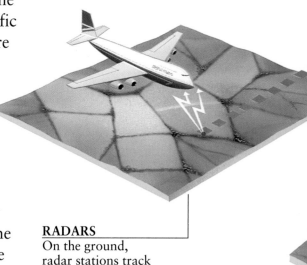

RADARS
On the ground, radar stations track each aircraft's progress.

KEEPING IN TOUCH
Modern airliners have sophisticated equipment which both receives and sends out signals. Most of this is hidden away beneath the body panelling.

 **LOOK OUT FOR THESE**

■ **FIELDS**
Seen from high above, different crops and colours can be seen.

■ **COASTLINES**
Waves breaking onto beaches form part of a long coastline.

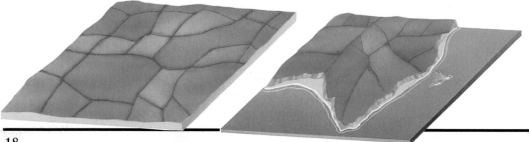

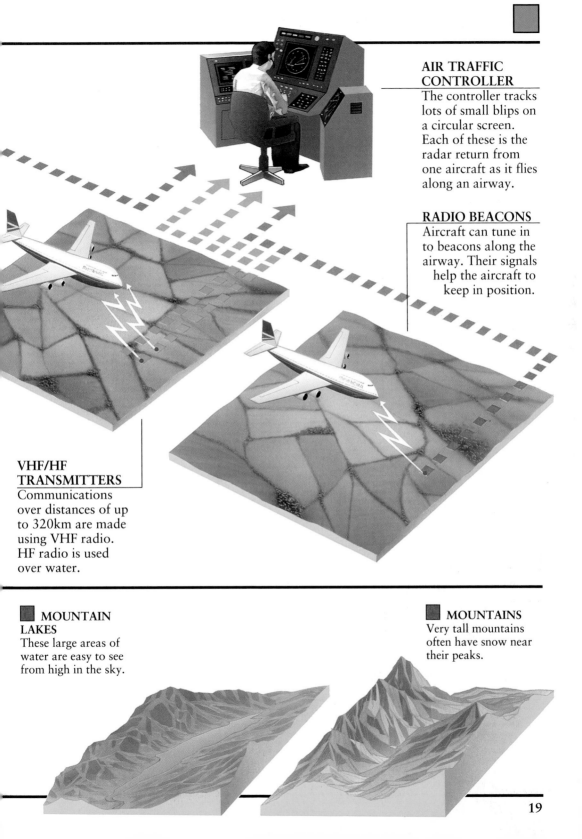

AIR TRAFFIC CONTROLLER
The controller tracks lots of small blips on a circular screen. Each of these is the radar return from one aircraft as it flies along an airway.

RADIO BEACONS
Aircraft can tune in to beacons along the airway. Their signals help the aircraft to keep in position.

VHF/HF TRANSMITTERS
Communications over distances of up to 320km are made using VHF radio. HF radio is used over water.

MOUNTAIN LAKES
These large areas of water are easy to see from high in the sky.

MOUNTAINS
Very tall mountains often have snow near their peaks.

LANDING

Approximately 30 minutes before arrival, the pilots prepare for the most dangerous part of the flight – landing. Speed is reduced and a descent is started. As the airliner gets closer to the airport, it is placed into a well-ordered landing pattern by an approach controller as other airliners may also be waiting to land. The flaps and undercarriage are lowered as the pilots concentrate hard on making a good approach and landing. Spoilers, autobrakes and thrust reversers help slow the airliner on the runway, and soon it is making its way to a gate at the end of the flight.

LANDING AIDS

There are two main systems of lights along runways (VASI and PAPI) to guide a pilot into land. He sees rows of red and white lights that tell him whether he is approaching at the correct angle.

FLAPS

Flaps on the back of the wing are lowered before landing. This helps the aircraft to lose height.

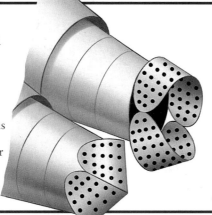

LOOK OUT FOR THESE

■ **THRUST REVERSERS**
To help the aircraft slow down after it has landed, doors called buckets clam together at the back of each engine. This deflects the exhaust forward.

move ahead

turn left

slow down

stop

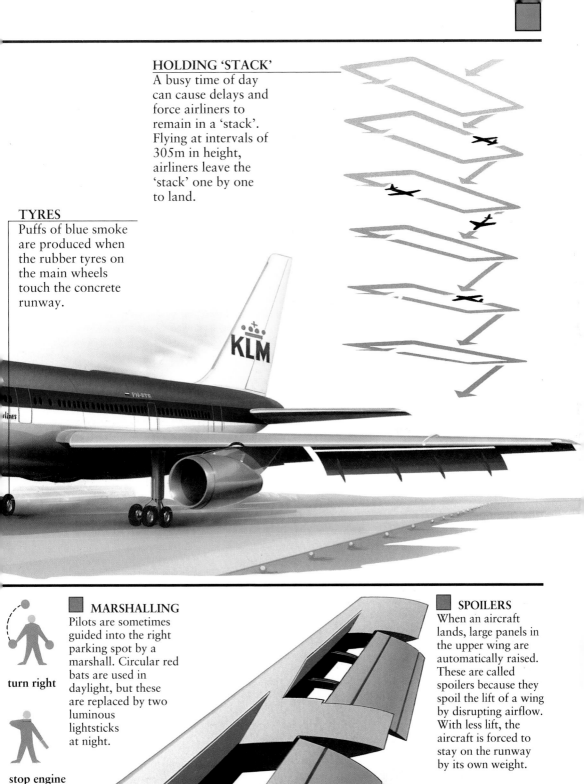

HOLDING 'STACK'
A busy time of day can cause delays and force airliners to remain in a 'stack'. Flying at intervals of 305m in height, airliners leave the 'stack' one by one to land.

TYRES
Puffs of blue smoke are produced when the rubber tyres on the main wheels touch the concrete runway.

KLM

MARSHALLING
Pilots are sometimes guided into the right parking spot by a marshall. Circular red bats are used in daylight, but these are replaced by two luminous lightsticks at night.

turn right

stop engine

SPOILERS
When an aircraft lands, large panels in the upper wing are automatically raised. These are called spoilers because they spoil the lift of a wing by disrupting airflow. With less lift, the aircraft is forced to stay on the runway by its own weight.

LARGE FOUR-ENGINED JETS

Four-engined jets include some of the world's largest and most powerful airliners. Most can carry hundreds of passengers for thousands of kilometres, on non-stop flights lasting up to 18 hours. Even bigger jets are planned for the future.

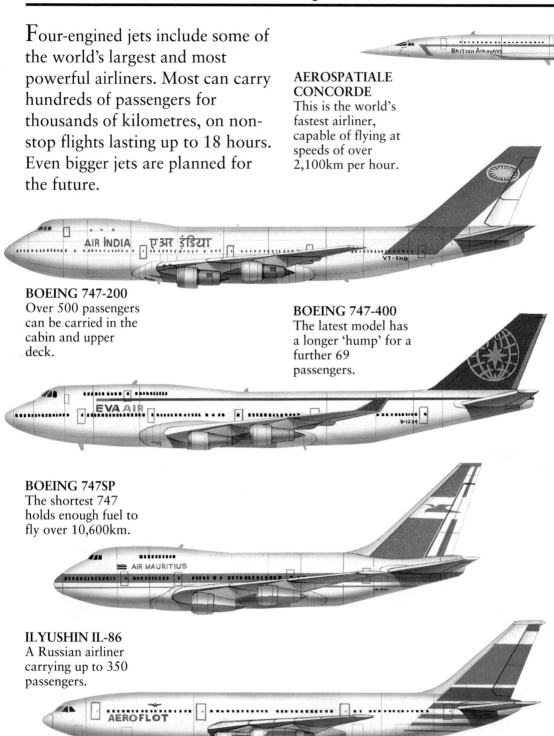

AEROSPATIALE CONCORDE
This is the world's fastest airliner, capable of flying at speeds of over 2,100km per hour.

BOEING 747-200
Over 500 passengers can be carried in the cabin and upper deck.

BOEING 747-400
The latest model has a longer 'hump' for a further 69 passengers.

BOEING 747SP
The shortest 747 holds enough fuel to fly over 10,600km.

ILYUSHIN IL-86
A Russian airliner carrying up to 350 passengers.

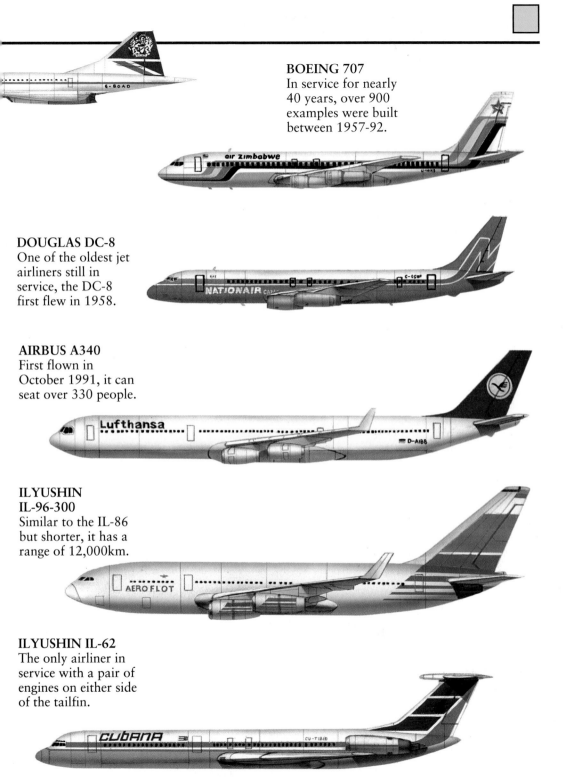

BOEING 707
In service for nearly 40 years, over 900 examples were built between 1957-92.

DOUGLAS DC-8
One of the oldest jet airliners still in service, the DC-8 first flew in 1958.

AIRBUS A340
First flown in October 1991, it can seat over 330 people.

ILYUSHIN IL-96-300
Similar to the IL-86 but shorter, it has a range of 12,000km.

ILYUSHIN IL-62
The only airliner in service with a pair of engines on either side of the tailfin.

LARGE TWO- AND THREE-ENGINED JETS

Many airlines do not carry enough passengers over long enough distances to justify using a large fleet of the very large four-engined jets. Instead, they use more economical two- and three-engined designs.

MCDONNELL DOUGLAS MD-11
US trijet which can seat 405.

AIRBUS A300
Over 400 have been built and delivered since its first flight in October 1972.

BOEING 767-300
This is longer than the 767-200 model.

LOCKHEED TRISTAR
Another US trijet, 249 of which have been delivered.

MCDONNELL DOUGLAS DC-10
A total of 386 were built between 1968-89.

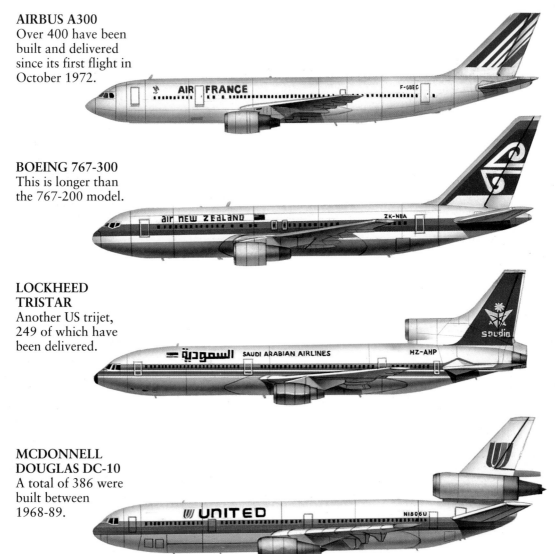

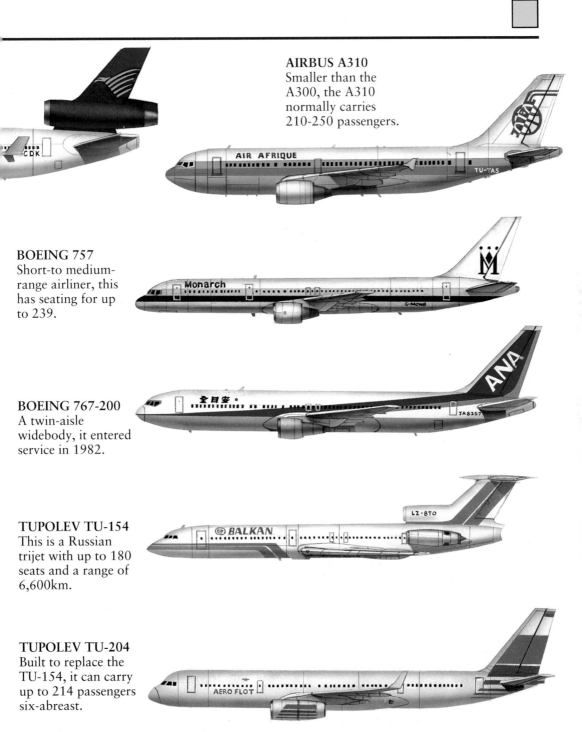

AIRBUS A310
Smaller than the
A300, the A310
normally carries
210-250 passengers.

AIR AFRIQUE

TU-TAS

BOEING 757
Short-to medium-
range airliner, this
has seating for up
to 239.

Monarch

G-MONB

BOEING 767-200
A twin-aisle
widebody, it entered
service in 1982.

全日空

JA8257

ANA

TUPOLEV TU-154
This is a Russian
trijet with up to 180
seats and a range of
6,600km.

BALKAN

LZ-BTO

TUPOLEV TU-204
Built to replace the
TU-154, it can carry
up to 214 passengers
six-abreast.

AERO FLOT

MEDIUM TWO-, THREE- & FOUR-ENGINED JETS

The most common jet in service with today's airlines is the short- to medium-range aircraft, seating an average of 130 passengers. These jets are the true workhorses of the airline world.

BOEING 727
No less than 1,832 examples were built, many of which are still in service.

MCDONNELL DOUGLAS MD-82
This is basically a stretched DC-9, with five-abreast seating for 172 passengers.

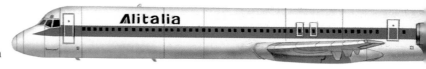

AIRBUS A320
Over 700 of the world's most advanced airliner have been ordered.

MCDONNELL DOUGLAS DC-9-32
A stretched version of the basic 90-seat DC-9. It has an extra 25 seats.

FOKKER 100
This Dutch design has a range of 3,167km.

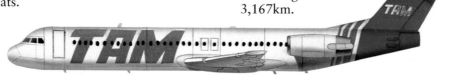

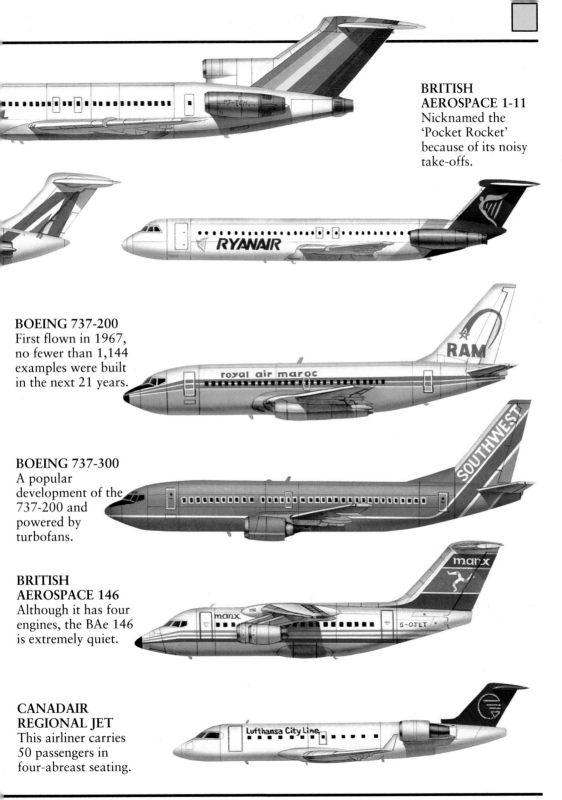

BRITISH AEROSPACE 1-11
Nicknamed the 'Pocket Rocket' because of its noisy take-offs.

BOEING 737-200
First flown in 1967, no fewer than 1,144 examples were built in the next 21 years.

BOEING 737-300
A popular development of the 737-200 and powered by turbofans.

BRITISH AEROSPACE 146
Although it has four engines, the BAe 146 is extremely quiet.

CANADAIR REGIONAL JET
This airliner carries 50 passengers in four-abreast seating.

TWIN PROP-ENGINED AIRCRAFT

Commuter aircraft became very popular during the 1980s. Small airlines flew quite small numbers of passengers over short distances. These flights often connect with intercontinental flights flown by the big airlines' larger jets.

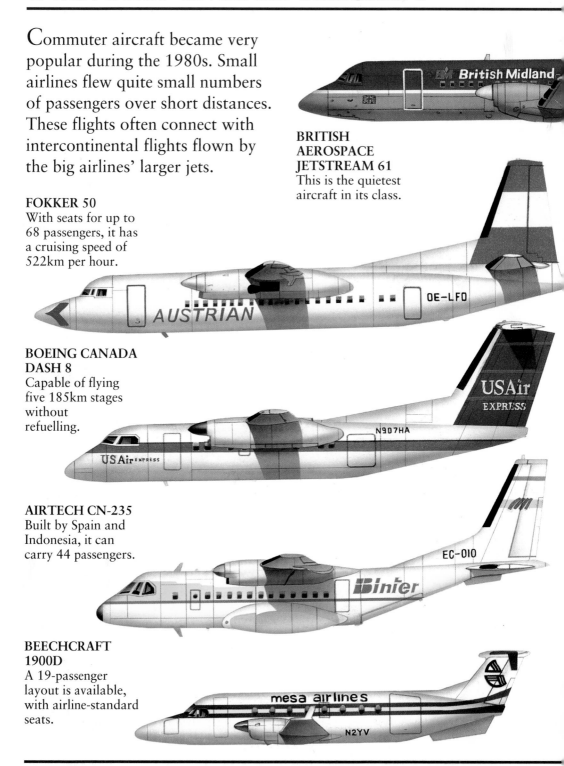

BRITISH AEROSPACE JETSTREAM 61
This is the quietest aircraft in its class.

FOKKER 50
With seats for up to 68 passengers, it has a cruising speed of 522km per hour.

BOEING CANADA DASH 8
Capable of flying five 185km stages without refuelling.

AIRTECH CN-235
Built by Spain and Indonesia, it can carry 44 passengers.

BEECHCRAFT 1900D
A 19-passenger layout is available, with airline-standard seats.

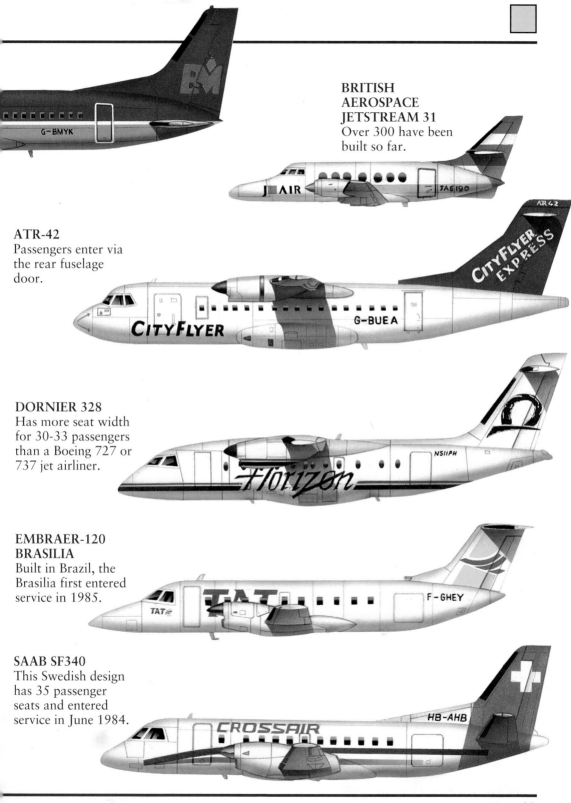

BRITISH AEROSPACE JETSTREAM 31
Over 300 have been built so far.

G-BMYK

J AIR   JA6190

ATR-42
Passengers enter via the rear fuselage door.

CITYFLYER   G-BUE A   CITYFLYER EXPRESS   ATR 42

DORNIER 328
Has more seat width for 30-33 passengers than a Boeing 727 or 737 jet airliner.

Horizon   N511PH

EMBRAER-120 BRASILIA
Built in Brazil, the Brasilia first entered service in 1985.

TAT   F-GHEY

SAAB SF340
This Swedish design has 35 passenger seats and entered service in June 1984.

CROSSAIR   HB-AHB

CARGO AIRCRAFT

While the vast majority of the world's airliners are used to carry passengers, some have been converted to carry cargo. In addition, some designs have been built especially to carry out this important task.

LOCKHEED ELECTRA
This is a version of a passenger aircraft that has had its seats removed.

BOEING 707
A large door in the fuselage ahead of the wing allows the cargo to be loaded.

SHORT BELFAST
In service with only one airline, the Belfast can lift a payload of 34,000kg.

LOCKHEED L-100-30 HERCULES
A US design based on a military transporter.

ANTONOV AN-124
Loading takes place via a rear ramp and a nose that hinges upwards.

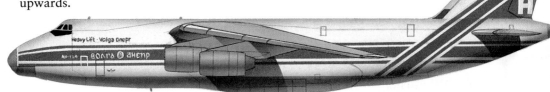

MCDONNELL DOUGLAS DC-10
Like the Boeing 707, it has a cargo door ahead of the wing.

FEDERAL EXPRESS

MCDONNELL DOUGLAS DC-8
Stripped of its seats, the cabin can carry a lot of cargo.

SOUTHERN AIR TRANSPORT

BOEING 757
Identified by the lack of passenger windows, it can carry 15 cargo pallets.

Zambia Airways

Iraqi

ILYUSHIN IL-76
Over 700 of these rear-loading Russian freighters have been built to date.

BOEING 747
This freighter has a nose which hinges upwards for loading and unloading.

cargolux

EXECUTIVE JETS

Although they are small and can carry only a few passengers, executive jets (also known as 'biz–jets') are the most comfortable aircraft to fly in. Fitted with specially made luxurious interiors, they are bought by companies and rich people.

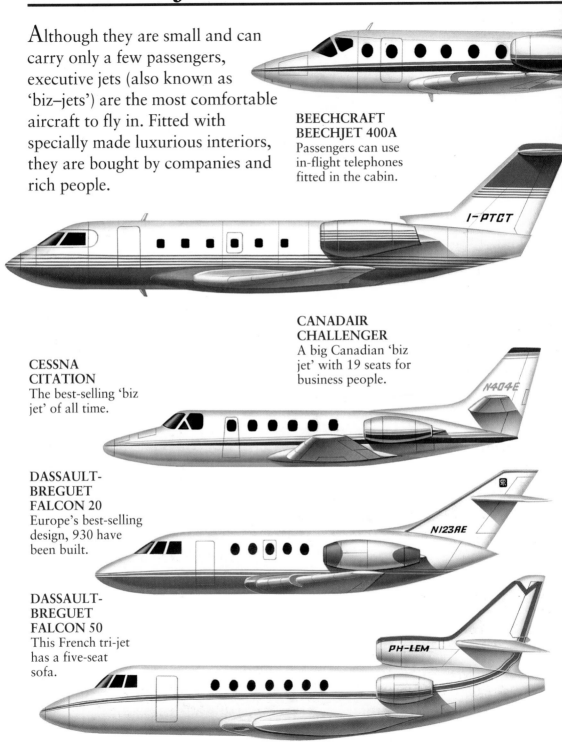

BEECHCRAFT BEECHJET 400A
Passengers can use in-flight telephones fitted in the cabin.

CANADAIR CHALLENGER
A big Canadian 'biz jet' with 19 seats for business people.

CESSNA CITATION
The best-selling 'biz jet' of all time.

DASSAULT-BREGUET FALCON 20
Europe's best-selling design, 930 have been built.

DASSAULT-BREGUET FALCON 50
This French tri-jet has a five-seat sofa.

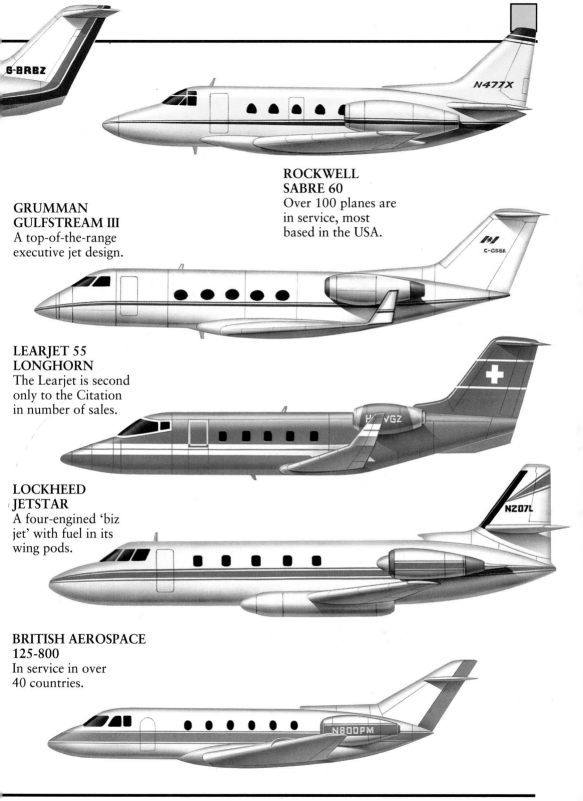

G-BRBZ

N477X

**ROCKWELL
SABRE 60**
Over 100 planes are
in service, most
based in the USA.

**GRUMMAN
GULFSTREAM III**
A top-of-the-range
executive jet design.

C-GSBR

**LEARJET 55
LONGHORN**
The Learjet is second
only to the Citation
in number of sales.

**LOCKHEED
JETSTAR**
A four-engined 'biz
jet' with fuel in its
wing pods.

N207L

**BRITISH AEROSPACE
125-800**
In service in over
40 countries.

N800PM

AIRLINE INSIGNIA

With airlines in service all over the world, it is not surprising that each airline wants to make its own aircraft easy to identify. The easiest and most colourful way to do this is to paint the airliners in a distinctive colour scheme, known as the livery. The most important part of the livery of an airliner is the tail insignia. These insignia usually include an airline's logo and the initials of its name, although sometimes the full name appears.

Air Zimbabwe

Alitalia

American Airlines

Austrian Airlines

Balkan Bulgarian

British Airways

British Midland

Cathay Pacific

Crossair

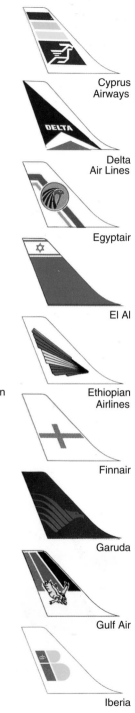

Cyprus Airways

Delta Air Lines

Egyptair

El Al

Ethiopian Airlines

Finnair

Garuda

Gulf Air

Iberia

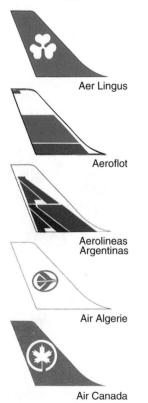

Aer Lingus

Aeroflot

Aerolineas Argentinas

Air Algerie

Air Canada

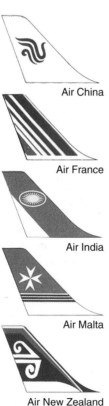

Air China

Air France

Air India

Air Malta

Air New Zealand

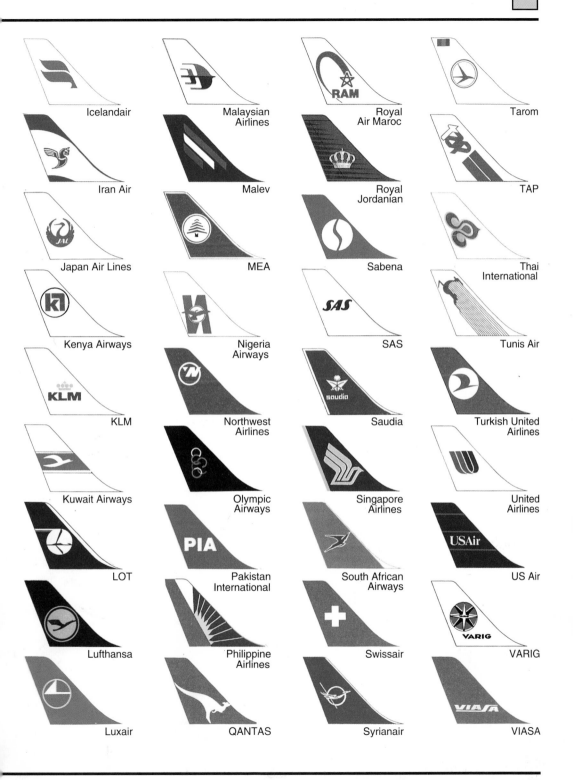

Icelandair	Malaysian Airlines	Royal Air Maroc	Tarom
Iran Air	Malev	Royal Jordanian	TAP
Japan Air Lines	MEA	Sabena	Thai International
Kenya Airways	Nigeria Airways	SAS	Tunis Air
KLM	Northwest Airlines	Saudia	Turkish United Airlines
Kuwait Airways	Olympic Airways	Singapore Airlines	United Airlines
LOT	Pakistan International	South African Airways	US Air
Lufthansa	Philippine Airlines	Swissair	VARIG
Luxair	QANTAS	Syrianair	VIASA

HELICOPTERS

Most aircraft have long wings on each side of the fuselage, which produce lift to help the aircraft fly. But a helicopter produces lift by using two or more long, thin 'wings' above the fuselage, known as rotor blades. They are turned at very high speed by the engine to produce lift, and their angle can be altered to make the helicopter fly in any direction or even hover. This makes the helicopter more versatile than normal aircraft.

MAIN ROTOR
To fly forwards, the whole main rotor of two or more blades is tilted forwards.

LANDING SKIDS
Many of the smaller, lighter helicopters land on long skids below the fuselage.

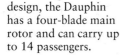

LOOK OUT FOR THESE

AEROSPATIALE DAUPHIN
A twin-engined French design, the Dauphin has a four-blade main rotor and can carry up to 14 passengers.

AEROSPATIALE ECUREUIL
Powered by a single engine, its three rotor blades are made out of glass fibre.

BELL 212
This American design has one engine which turns a main rotor with only two blades.

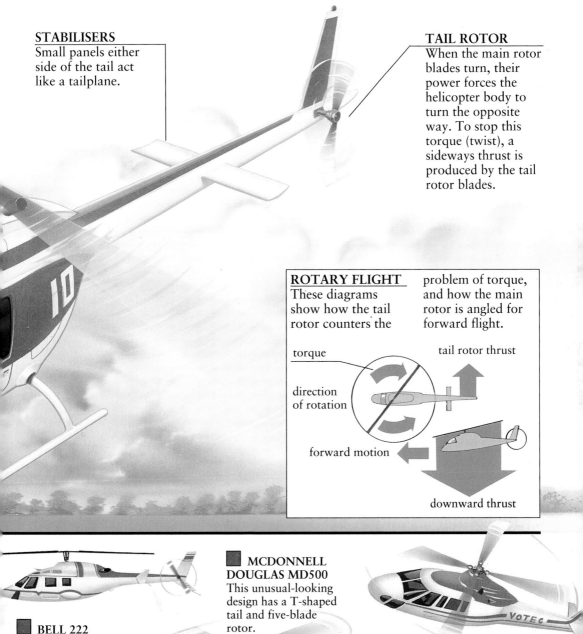

STABILISERS
Small panels either side of the tail act like a tailplane.

TAIL ROTOR
When the main rotor blades turn, their power forces the helicopter body to turn the opposite way. To stop this torque (twist), a sideways thrust is produced by the tail rotor blades.

ROTARY FLIGHT
These diagrams show how the tail rotor counters the problem of torque, and how the main rotor is angled for forward flight.

torque

direction of rotation

tail rotor thrust

forward motion

downward thrust

MCDONNELL DOUGLAS MD500
This unusual-looking design has a T-shaped tail and five-blade rotor.

BELL 222
The main wheels are carried in small wings located on each side of the fuselage.

SIKORSKY SPIRIT
The main wheels can be retracted into the lower fuselage of this 14-seater.

ENGINES

The engines of a jet airliner work by sucking in air at the front, compressing it, then mixing it with burning fuel. The hot air expands rapidly and is forced backwards and out as a very powerful exhaust. Ideally, the engines of an airliner should be reliable, powerful, quiet, clean and fuel-efficient. Turbofan engines are best for high subsonic speeds, but turboprop engines are better suited for the slower speeds and shorter flights.

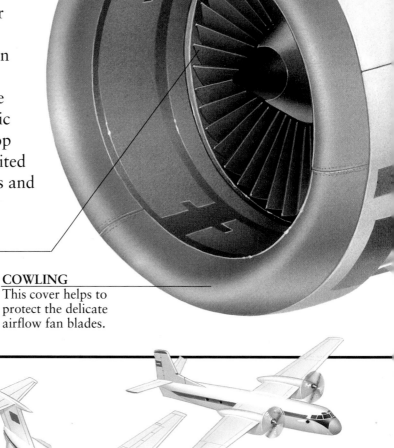

AIRFLOW FAN
Much of the air the fan sucks in is bypassed around the engine and mixed with the exhaust to produce more thrust.

COWLING
This cover helps to protect the delicate airflow fan blades.

LOOK OUT FOR THESE

ANTONOV AN-72
This is a Russian transport aircraft which is powered by two turbofan engines. These extend ahead of the high wing.

ANTONOV AN-32
Like the AN-72, the engines of the AN-32 are above and ahead of the wing, but they are turboprops.

EXHAUST NOZZLE
The air passes out of the nozzle at high speed to form thrust.

TURBOJET
Lots of thrust from the exhaust is ideal for supersonic travel.

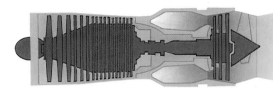

TURBOPROP
A gas turbine drives a propeller at the front via a gearbox.

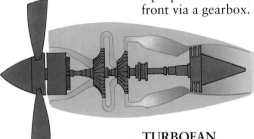

TURBINE
The hot air turns a turbine which drives the air compressors and airflow fan.

TURBOFAN
Efficient at high subsonic speeds, they are fitted to many airliners.

COMBUSTION CHAMBER
Compressed air and burning fuel are mixed here.

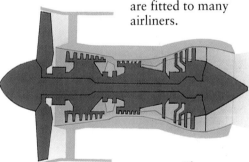

 PIAGGIO AVANTI
The two turboprops are rear-facing and are called pushers.

 PBN TRISLANDER
This is an unusual aircraft because it has one of its three piston engines at the top of the fin.

CESSNA SKYMASTER
One engine facing the front and one facing the back makes this what is called a 'push me, pull me' aircraft.

GLIDERS

Most aircraft have one or more engines for power, but gliders are very different. These aircraft glide through the air without the help of engines, using currents of rising hot air called thermals to help them stay up in the sky. The wings are long to produce lots of lift from the airflow, and the whole glider is as streamlined as possible.

Gliders are towed up into the air either by powered aircraft or by long winches from the ground.

AIRBRAKES
These help to reduce speed and height by creating drag when raised into the air.

CANOPY
The canopy covering the cockpit is often tinted to reduce the sun's glare and heat.

LANDING WHEEL
Some modern gliders are fitted with a large wheel to help them land smoothly.

LOOK OUT FOR THESE

TWO SEATER
Gliders with seats for two are used to train new pilots. An instructor can sit in the rear seat.

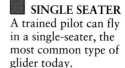

SINGLE SEATER
A trained pilot can fly in a single-seater, the most common type of glider today.

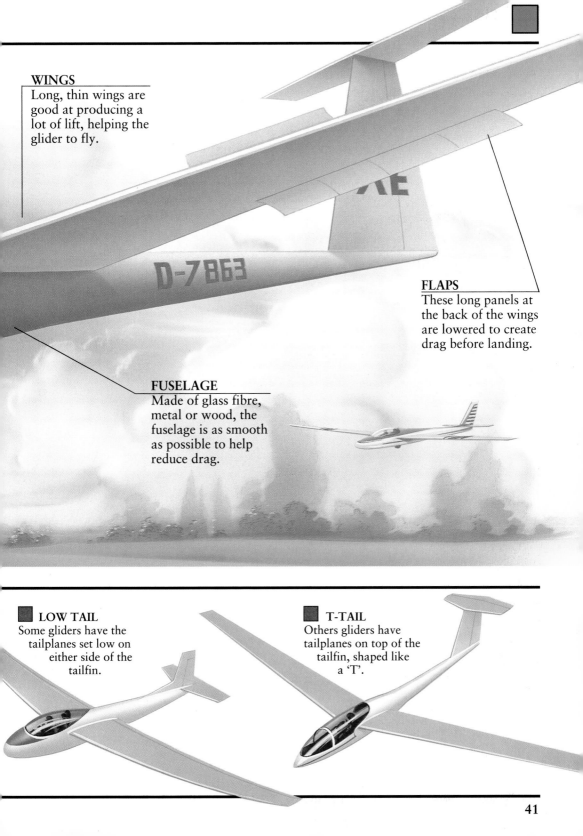

WINGS
Long, thin wings are good at producing a lot of lift, helping the glider to fly.

FLAPS
These long panels at the back of the wings are lowered to create drag before landing.

FUSELAGE
Made of glass fibre, metal or wood, the fuselage is as smooth as possible to help reduce drag.

LOW TAIL
Some gliders have the tailplanes set low on either side of the tailfin.

T-TAIL
Others gliders have tailplanes on top of the tailfin, shaped like a 'T'.

UNUSUAL AIRCRAFT

Although most of the aircraft illustrated in this book are large airliners built to carry passengers, there are many more types of aircraft, big and small, which are designed to carry out different tasks. Some look quite extraordinary.

FLS OPTICA
Observation plane which has an 'insect eye' cabin, giving all-round vision.

CESSNA STATIONAIR
This has floats so it can land on, and take-off from, water.

CANADAIR CL-215
It scoops up water, then takes off to drop the water on forest fires.

FFT SPEED CANARD
This small sports plane has two seats and a nosewheel which retracts.

AERO SPACELINES SUPER GUPPY
This strange-looking aircraft transports huge airliner wings.

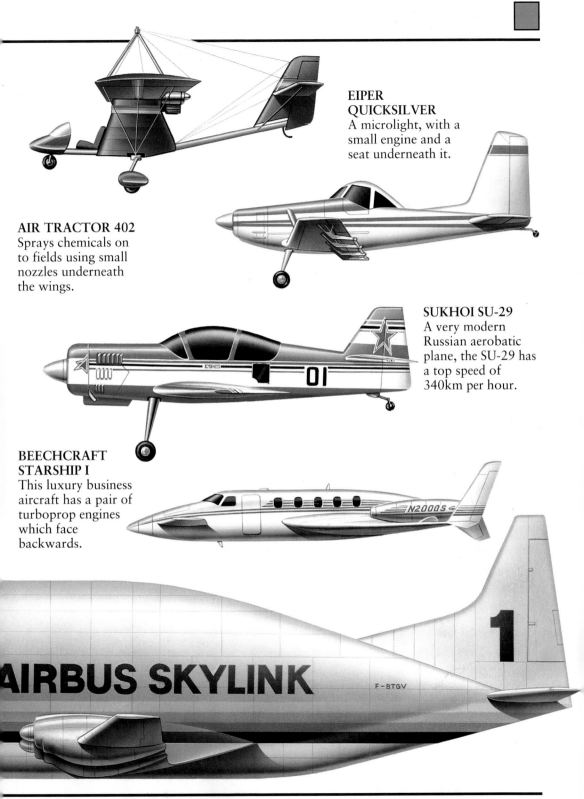

EIPER QUICKSILVER
A microlight, with a small engine and a seat underneath it.

AIR TRACTOR 402
Sprays chemicals on to fields using small nozzles underneath the wings.

SUKHOI SU-29
A very modern Russian aerobatic plane, the SU-29 has a top speed of 340km per hour.

BEECHCRAFT STARSHIP I
This luxury business aircraft has a pair of turboprop engines which face backwards.

AIRBUS SKYLINK

F-BTGV

GLOSSARY

Words in SMALL CAPITAL letters indicate a cross-reference.

airflow The movement of air over and under a surface, such as a wing. If airflow is smooth over the wing, LIFT will be created by a reduction in air pressure (lower above the wing than below it).

air corridor A 'corridor' of air space between airports which can only be entered by aircraft in radio contact with air traffic control

autobrakes Strong brakes on the undercarriage which activate automatically once the wheels have touched down on a RUNWAY.

'biz jet' A nickname for the executive jet, because most of those in use are owned and operated by businesses.

CAT III Abbreviation for Category III conditions which occur when visibility is very poor due to bad weather, such as fog. Some RUNWAYS have special sensors that can guide an aircraft in to land in these conditions.

cockpit The compartment at the front of an aircraft from where the pilots fly the aircraft. All flight controls and instruments are in the cockpit, also known as the flight deck.

control yoke The large column in front of the pilot's seat. It is moved forwards and backwards to make the aircraft descend or ascend, and left or right to make it move to the sides.

drag A force created by the resistance of AIRFLOW to a less than smooth object, such as a badly designed aircraft. Just as LIFT will force an object to rise, so DRAG will force the object to slow down.

flaps Movable sections at the back of a wing. They can be extended backwards to increase LIFT on take-off and deflected down to increase DRAG before landing.

fuel bowser A tanker lorry that can carry thousands of litres of fuel. It is used to refuel aircraft.

fuselage The main part of the body of an aircraft.

gate The place in the airport building where passengers enter and exit an aircraft, usually via an elevated walkway linked to a door in the aircraft's cabin.

helipad An area which is reserved for helicopters to land and take-off. It is usually marked by a large 'H'.

HF Abbreviation for 'High Frequency' radio waves.

holding point A position on the TAXIWAY close to the RUNWAY, where an aircraft waits for permission to enter the RUNWAY before take-off.

lift The upward force on a wing, created by the AIRFLOW passing over it. The faster and smoother the airflow, the greater the lift created.

main rotor The long, thin blades (usually from two to five in number) above a helicopter. On rotation at high speed, the blades create LIFT.

nosewheel The set of wheels at the front of an aircraft.

PAPI Abbreviation for 'Precision Approach Path Indicator' system which has four lights on each side of the runway to guide the pilot in to land at the right angle on the RUNWAY.

pre-flight checks Carried out before an aircraft ever takes off, these include checking that the flaps move correctly; that the engines are powering up smoothly and not overheating; and that all of the instruments in the COCKPIT are in working order.

radar A system used to send out a series of short radio waves which are reflected by any object they may strike, so giving away its position and movement.

runway The long, wide strip of concrete used by airliners when taking off and landing.

slats These long sections at the front of a wing can be moved forward and down (together with the FLAPS at the rear of the wing) to help create both LIFT and DRAG for take-off and landing respectively.

speed of sound This varies with height: 1,223km per hour at sea level; 1,090km per hour at 9,150m.

spoilers Long panels in a wing, raised to disrupt the AIRFLOW. This increases DRAG and reduces LIFT, so the aircraft can reduce speed and descend prior to landing. They are also known as airbrakes and speedbrakes.

subsonic speed A speed lower than that of the SPEED OF SOUND.

supersonic speed A speed higher than that of the SPEED OF SOUND.

taxiway The long concrete 'roads' at an airport used by airliners to move to and from a RUNWAY and a GATE.

thrust Pushing force created by an engine.

torque Twisting or turning caused by the rotation of blades, as in a helicopter.

tugs Vehicles that push or pull aircraft into and out of awkward areas, such as GATES, at an airport.

turbofan A TURBOJET engine with a large fan at the front to suck in the air. Unlike a turbojet, a proportion of the air is passed around the engine and released into the exhaust.

turbojet An engine in which greater THRUST is created by compressing all of the air sucked in and mixing all of it with burning fuel.

turboprop An engine on propeller-driven aircraft, it has a gas turbine whose extra power is geared down to drive (turn) the propeller fixed at the front of the engine unit.

undercarriage The main wheels of an aircraft, either under the wing or the FUSELAGE.

VASI Abbreviation for 'Visual Approach Slope Indicator'. This is a series of four bars of lights by the touchdown point of a RUNWAY which helps the pilot to judge the angle at which the plane is approaching the runway.

VHF Abbreviation for 'Very High Frequency' radio waves.

INDEX